DATE DUE

JUL 1 8 2006	
MAR 2 9 '07	
MAY 04 '07	
FEB 0 3 '09	
OCT 2 4 '10	
DEC 1 '10	
MAY 1 6 '11	
DEC 0 8 '11	
JUN 2 5 '12	
OCT 1 5 '12	

CUB TO GRIZZLY

ANIMALS GROWING UP

Jason Cooper

Rourke
Publishing LLC
Vero Beach, Florida 32964

© 2004 Rourke Publishing LLC

All rights reserved. No part of this book may be reproduced or utilized in any form or by any means, electronic or mechanical including photocopying, recording, or by any information storage and retrieval system without permission in writing from the publisher.

www.rourkepublishing.com

PHOTO CREDITS: All photos © Lynn M. Stone except pp. 8, 17 © Tom and Pat Leeson

Title page: *Now on its own, a blond three-year old cub fills up on greens.*

Editor: Frank Sloan

Cover design by Nicola Stratford

Library of Congress Cataloging-in-Publication Data

Cooper, Jason, 1942-
 Cub to grizzly / Jason Cooper.
   p. cm. — (Animals growing up)
 Includes bibliographical references (p.   ).
 Contents: Grizzly bears — Newborn cubs — Cubs growing up.
  ISBN 1-58952-691-0 (hardcover)
 1. Grizzly bear--Infancy--Juvenile literature. [1. Grizzly bear. 2. Bears. 3. Animals--Infancy.] I. Title. II Series: Cooper, Jason, ≠ d 1942-   Animals growing up.
  QL737.C27C666 2003
  599.784—dc21

2003007268

Printed in the USA

CG/CG

Table of Contents

Grizzly Bears	5
Newborn Cubs	6
Cubs Growing Up	14
Glossary	23
Index	24
Further Reading	24
Websites to Visit	24

Grizzly Bears

The largest grizzly, or brown, bears are the biggest of North America's meat-eating animals. These are the brown bears of Kodiak and nearby islands in Alaska.

Grizzlies are tremendously powerful animals. And despite their heavy bodies, they are very fast.

North American grizzlies live in a variety of **habitats** from Arctic **tundra** to forests, mountain meadows, and grassy seashores.

Grizzlies of coastal Alaska fatten up on summer salmon.

Newborn Cubs

A grizzly begins life in a dry, dark den. It may be the only cub, or it may be one of as many as four.

A grizzly mom gives birth while she is in a deep winter sleep called **hibernation**. The cubs are tiny at birth, weighing from just 12 ounces (340 grams) to 24 ounces (680 grams). They are born between January and March.

A mother nervously leads her triplets to a stream.

The cubs are not only small, but they are also quite helpless. Their **instincts**, however, are strong. They snuggle against their mother for warmth. They find her milk to satisfy their hunger.

The grizzly mother ends her hibernation in the spring. The cubs are now old enough to play outside the den and sample nearby plants.

It's playtime for grizzly twins in a Montana meadow.

By the age of three months the cubs are old enough to follow their mother. By watching and following, the cubs learn how and where to find food. They also learn about danger.

A grizzly mother is the cubs' "big brother" as well their teacher. She is fearless. If she must, she will defend her cubs against people or big male bears.

A mother grizzly growls at a male bear along a stream.

Adult male grizzlies are loners. They have no role in raising cubs. But they sometimes attack and kill cubs. Such attacks provide the males with food. But they also reduce the chances of "new" bears some day invading the male's home range.

Adult male grizzlies spend most of their time by themselves.

Cubs Growing Up

Grizzly cubs follow their mother like shadows. But when mom catches a salmon or other **prey**, it is every bear for itself. The mother bear does not tear up prey and divide it among her cubs. Each youngster quickly learns it must take what it wants.

Whatever this cub wants, it will have to take when the mother drags it ashore.

Although they are called **carnivores**, grizzlies eat a variety of foods. In spring, grizzlies along the coasts of Alaska and British Columbia dine on dead seals and whales. Later in the year, the bears find fresh new plants and roots. In late summer and fall the bears gobble up berries.

As **predators**, grizzlies kill animals such as ground squirrels and young caribou, mountain sheep, and deer. In coastal areas of Alaska and Canada, salmon are an important part of a grizzly's diet.

A grizzly cub in Montana learns from its mother how to dig roots for a meal.

In fact, a diet rich in salmon helps explain why **coastal** grizzlies weigh up to 1,700 pounds (773 kilograms). Elsewhere in North America, grizzlies may weigh as little as 210 pounds (95 kg).

Becoming a big **bruin** doesn't happen quickly. In southern Alaska, male grizzlies continue to grow even at 10 and 11 years of age. Cubs stay with their mother until they are at least two years old. Some stay with mom for as many as four years.

By watching its mother, this grizzly cub has learned how to grab salmon.

Young bears often travel with other young bears. But by age five or six, they are old enough to be fathers and mothers. The adult males will largely live alone, except when courting females. Females, too, live alone, except when they have cubs. However, when salmon fishing is good, grizzlies share the streams with each other.

Grizzlies that reach adulthood in North America have a fair chance of living long lives. Some grizzlies have been known to live into their 30s.

Now on their own, two young bears rest in a meadow.

On the alert, a mother grizzly stands to sniff for danger.

Glossary

bruin (BROO uhn) — nickname for any bear

carnivores (CAR nuh vorz) — meat-eating animals

coastal (COHS tul) — having to do with seashores (coasts)

habitats (HAB uh tatz) — special kinds of places where animals live, such as a mountain meadow or grassy seashore

hibernation (hy bur NAY shun) — a deep winter sleep in which an animal's body functions, like breathing, slow down

instincts (IN stinkz) — actions or behaviors with which an animal is born rather than which it learns

predators (PRED uht urz) — animals that hunt other animals for food

prey (PRAY) — an animal that is hunted by another animal for food

tundra (TUN druh) — a huge, treeless and dry area of the Far North with permanently frozen soil and a ground cover of low-lying plants

Index

den   6, 9
food   13, 16
habitat   5
hibernation   6, 9
males   11, 13, 20

mother   6, 9, 11, 14, 19, 20
predators   16
prey   14
salmon   16, 19

Further Reading

Deady, Kathleen W. *Grizzly Bears*. Capstone, 2002
Hall, Eleanor J. *Grizzly*. Kidhaven Press, 2001

Websites To Visit

www.wildlifesearch.com/bear.htm
www.pbs.org/wnet/nature/grizzlies/river.html

About The Author

Jason Cooper has written several children's books about a variety of topics for Rourke Publishing, including the recent series *Eye to Eye With Big Cats* and *Holiday Celebrations.* Cooper travels widely to gather information for his books. Two of his favorite travel destinations are Alaska and the Far East.